the EARTHWORM BOOK

by Alicia Previn

The Earthworm Book (Second Edition)
Written and illustrated by Alicia Previn

Copyright © 2008 by Alicia Previn

All rights reserved. Under International Copyright Law, no part of this publication may be reproduced, stored, transmitted by any means - electronic, mechanical, photographic (photocopy), recording, or otherwise - without written permission from the publisher.

Library of Congress Catalog Card Number: T.B.A.
International Standard Book Number 978-0-9847107-0-6

Printed in the United States of America.

Dedication

For Peter Dukich, master gardener, teacher, friend, lover of his fellow man and earthworms.

"The seeds that fell on the good soil represent honest, good-hearted people who hear God's word, cling to it, and patiently produce a huge harvest." (NLT) Luke 8:15

We are special little people, human beings, living on this very large planet called Earth. We live in a city full of people, where we have an important job to do growing and learning, but we are just one of many, and sometimes that makes us feel small, too small to be important. Well, down beneath the surface of the earth there is a living creature much, much smaller than any of us, who also has a very important job caring for the earth, called the earthworm.

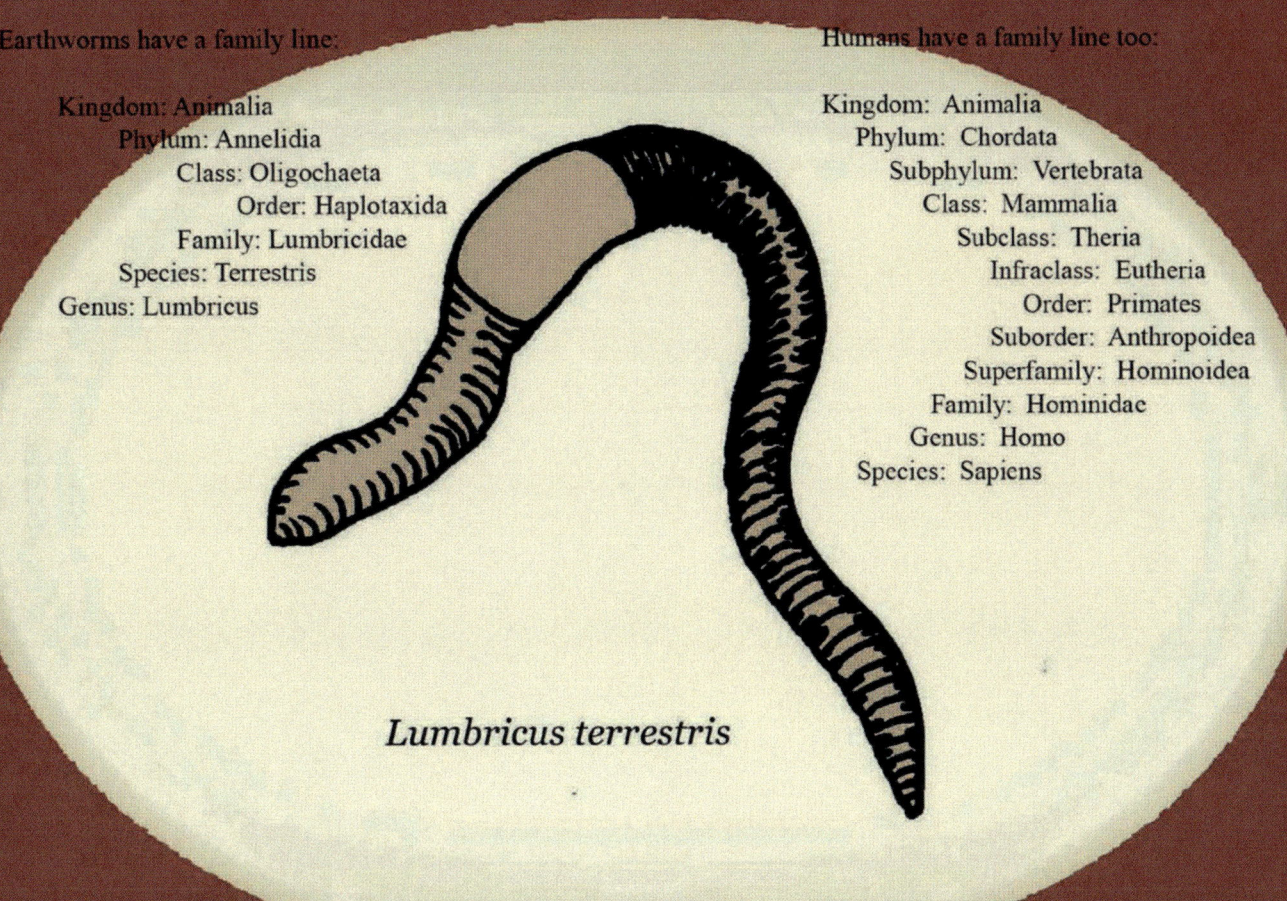

hey work hard everyday taking dirt and changing it into rich, healthy living soil that helps plants grow and bloom, providing everyone with food.

arthworms like to be down in their tunnels that they dig with their mouth, working where it is dark and damp. They come up to the surface to pick up fallen leaves, pulling them by the stem down underground to grind up and change into soil. If you see them out of the ground help them get back down into the soil, they may have been washed out by rain water.

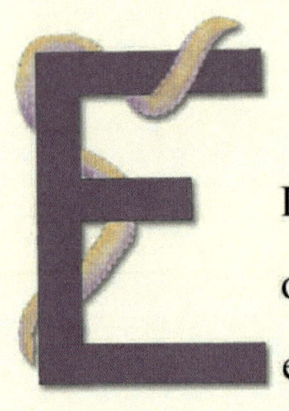earthworms do this amazing job of changing organic garbage into soil without having a nose, eyes, or ears, simply a mouth with no teeth for eating dirt that passes through their body, turning it into something of great value, like gold!

Let's think of all the things we can do with our eyes, ears, and nose.

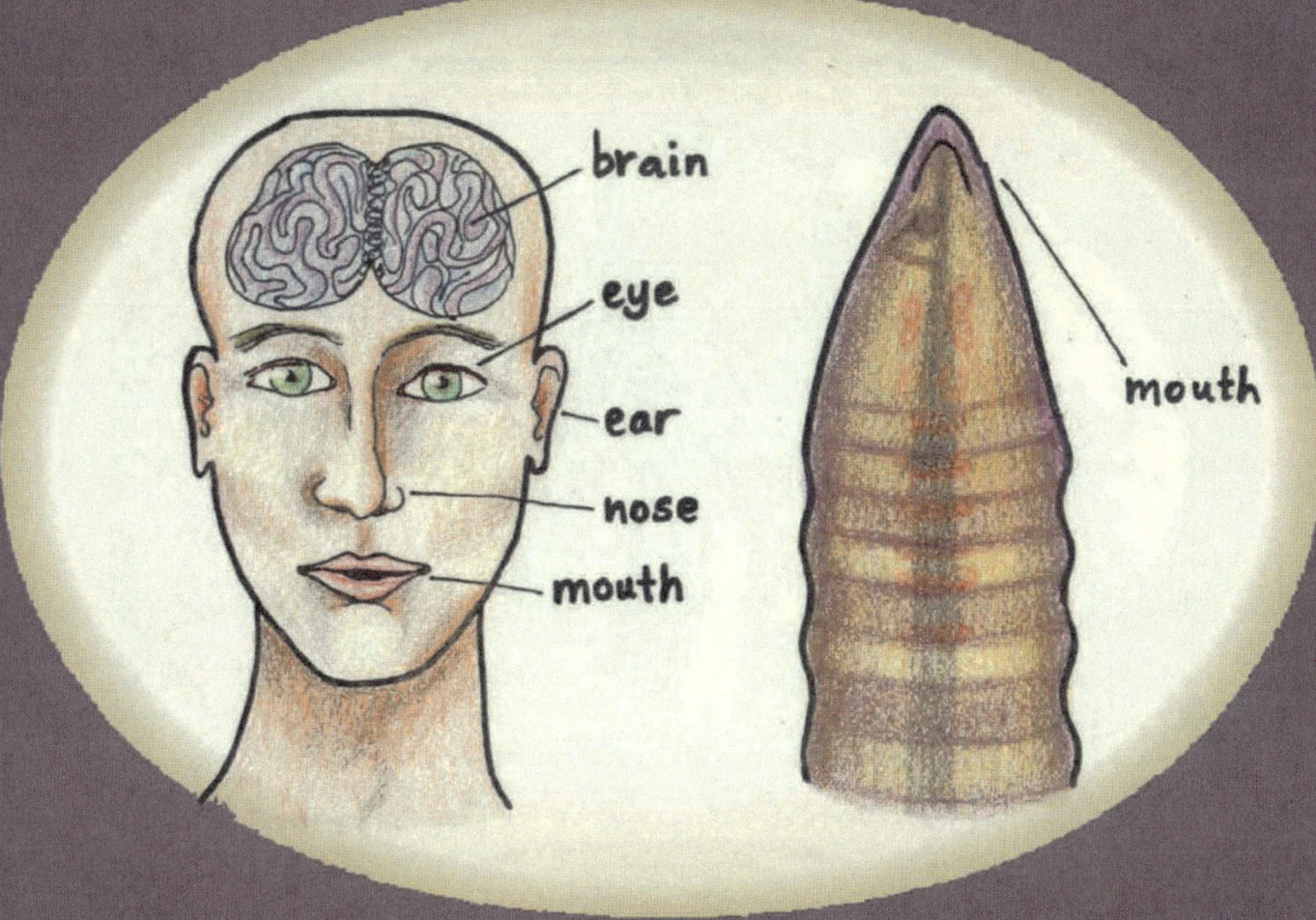

When someone is digging with a shovel and can't see that a worm is working there, it can happen, accidentally, that a worm is cut in two. Ouch! Earthworms have long bodies that are very special as each part can *heal where they were cut and can continue to live. They are completely harmless.

*a worm's body can regenerate but they do not become two worms

Earthworms are one of very few creatures that lay eggs by being both Mom and Dad at the same time. Their one purpose is to care for the soil and earth; it's all they do and you will find them all across the world. How is this possible for one so small? The very first worms lived in one place and their eggs traveled on the bottoms of walking shoes and horses' hooves for thousands of years, spreading them everywhere.

Many people think of worms just for fishing and use them as bait to put on a fish-hook because they are a tasty food for a fish. Now that we know about the important work they do, they don't seem so small at all or lowly; their life is big, as big as 1000 feet tall to the dirt, the Earth, and all animals and humans.

he Earthworm's life is about making things better, as they give everything for me and for you and care with all they have: we want to love them and treat them nicely. Earthworms, you are not dirty, you're precious! Send a kiss to one today!

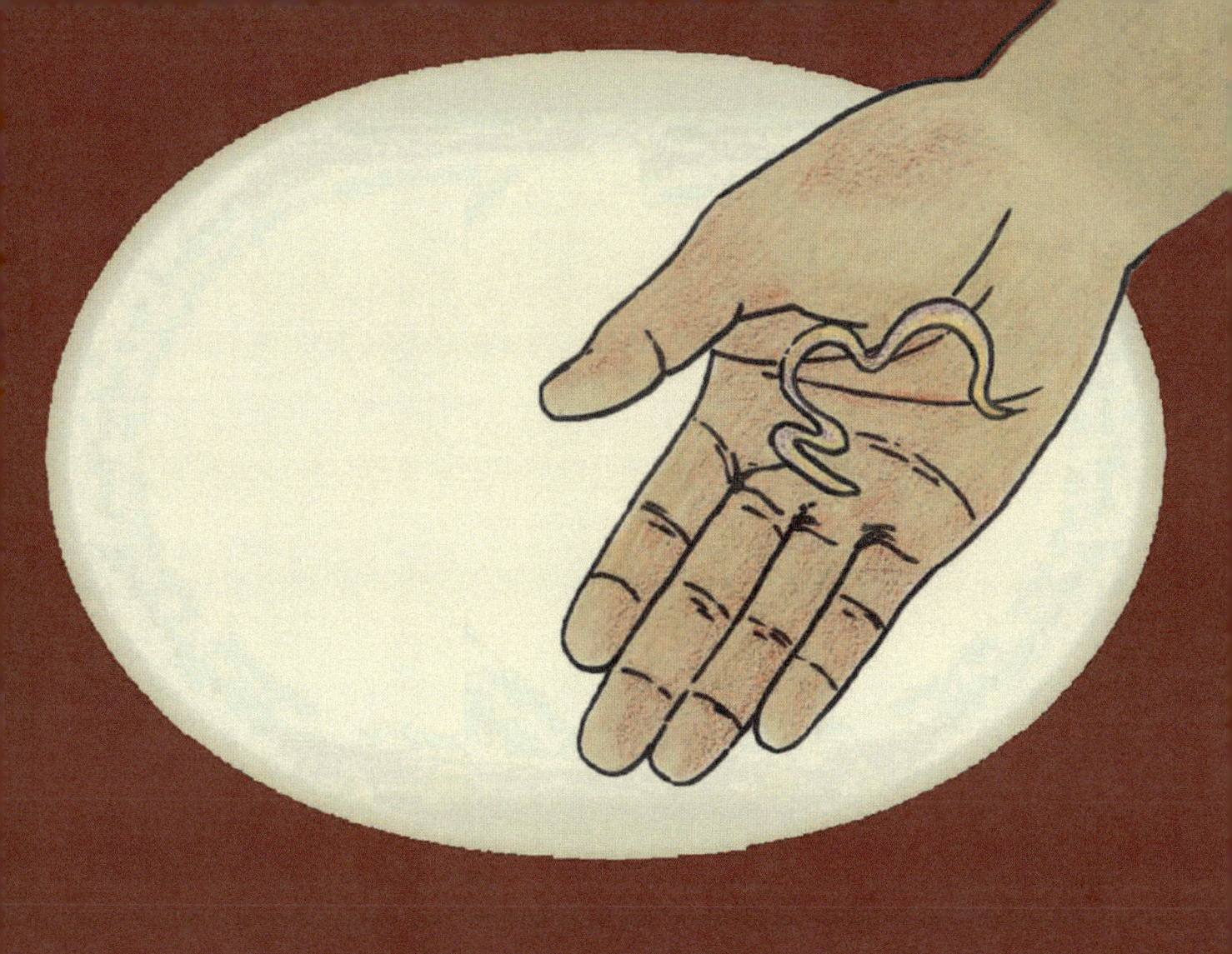

EARTHWORM

Great beauty beneath the soil where the earthworms lay

A reason to live and work, each and everyday

Turning the soil into gold, precious enough to hold...

Earthworm, you make us humans small

Earthworm, you make us humans small

No need for eyes or ears, but you are the smartest of all

Watch out! though a spade may sever, you are a perfect mender...

Earthworm, you make us kids look small

Earthworm, you make us kids look small

Male and female you are exclusive to this gender

The earth is moved by your sole purpose,

Can't call you lowly, for you life is a thousand feet tall

You make us all look small!

If I could walk the earth, my shoes would carry your secret worth

To creatures great and small they know that soon you'll have food for us all

Your life is a towering sacrifice, I want to love you, and treat you nice!

Earthworm, you make us kids look small

Earthworm, you make us humans small

Great beauty beneath the soil where the Earthworms lay...

How You Can Care for Them...

Make Your Own
(for the thrifty do-it-yourself person):

You can build your own worm farm with two identical plastic containers, minimum 1-foot depth, that stack into one another leaving 2-3 inch gap in the bottom, and a well-fitting lid. Use a drill to pierce the upper container along the sides for drainage; about 2 inches above the bottom. Place upper container inside the lower container and prepare for your worms: You will need a newspaper or cardboard torn into strips for bedding which you spread thickly across the bottom. Sprinkle it with garden soil to cover it lightly. Water it until moist but not soggy and leave for 2 days until it is ready for your worms. Add worms (availability by mail online from the below websites) and *food; place the lid loosely over the top.

*Begin saving food scraps from your kitchen or garden, especially fruit and vegetable waste crushed eggshells, tea leaves, fish bones, coffee grounds(worms like to lay their eggs in it), leftovers. NO garlic, onion, leeks, or citrus. Distribue a little every few days on top of the soil and watch them transform it! Remember worms like dark so they will spend most of their time below in the bedding.
For further information or questions
conact me: alicia@earthwormbook.com

You can Buy or Make a Worm Growing Box to enrich your soil for plants or gardens, and use up kitchen food waste.
Have fun with your own worms!

The ultimate Worm Growing Box: Gusanito Worm Bin Farm.
No odor, indoor/outdoor, low maintenance. Available online from many sources, including www.WormsWrangler.com

Earthworm Nurseries: Watch them hatch and
grow in their own little decorative tent! Available from
www.unclejimswormfarm.com
www.naturepavilion.com

Acknowledgments

Story/Concept: Alicia Previn
Illustrations: Alicia Previn
Early Edits: Peggy Stevers of Stevers Design and Oliver Ybarra

Music Credits:

"Earthworm Song" written by Alicia Previn (1993 Lovely Previn Music/ASCAP)

"Let's Get Acquainted" written by David Ybarra (2008 Modern Bakery Music/ASCAP)

"Anatomy Class" written by David Ybarra (2008 Modern Bakery Music/ASCAP)

"The Salesman and The Horsee" written by David Ybarra (2008 Modern Bakery Music/ASCAP)

"Do The Wiggle" written by David Ybarra (2008 Modern Bakery Musci/ASCAP)

Music Selections Produced by David Ybarra/The Modern Bakery Studio
San Diego, CA

Special Thanks to: *The Author of Love.*
MTC who was inspired by love. Max, my son who has heard the song the most!

Made in the USA
Coppell, TX
20 January 2026

69545980R00017